The ABC's of Transgender

Keys to a Deeper Understanding of Gender identity and Sexual Identity

Lauren A. McMann

ISBN-13: 978-1978489998

ISBN-10: 1978489994

DEDICATION

This book is dedicated to raising awareness of
discrimination faced by transgender people!

TABLE OF CONTENT

INTRODUCTION

Your sexual reception and gender identity are important part of who you are. Having a deeper understanding about gender identity, gender, and sexual orientation goes a long way to help you understand who you truly are and the world around you.

The word Transgender should not be mistaken for LGBT, they are two different terms with different meanings. A transgender person feels like the sex assigned to him or her is different from what he or she chooses to identify with and therefore goes all out to change the present gender state to a new one while the LGBT does not involve changing vital organs in the body.

Gender Identity is all about who you really are. It describes your person and this is what people on the outside take you to be.

There are many different terms used in describing those in the transgender community which includes, queer, transgender, transsexual, non-binary, and many others.

The LGBT falls under the umbrella of sexual orientation. Sexual orientation describes the people and things you are attracted to and who you would like to have relationships with. It should also be noted that this sexual orientation is different from gender and gender identity. You should understand the meanings of each so you can easily distinguish when you are involved in communications about them. The latter is not about whom you are attracted to or not, it is about your personality, the real you – female, male, genderqueer, etc.

For clarity, sexual orientation is all about who you want to be associated with while gender identity is about who you truly are.

Lauren's Tip: This is available on the last page of this book.

Chapter 1

Meaning of Transgender

Transgender is a word with dynamic meanings. It means a person whose personal identity and gender identity does not align with their birth sex. This word refers to the set of people who moved away from their assigned gender at birth. Those who do this do so because they probably feel they belong to another gender where they believe and expect they would function better.

For the purpose of this book, we will break down the word "transgender." Trans means "change" while gender means a "societal definition of sex." These individuals do not have a drive to change their sex. They are content with their physical bodies, they just prefer to behave, dress or otherwise identify as the opposite gender publically.

This term is not to be confused with "cross-dressers" or "transvestites". Cross-dressers are those that enjoy wearing clothing or altering their physical appearance to that of the opposite gender for pleasure or entertainment (as in Drag Queens). This is a fine line, and even in the trans community the definitions are still up for discussion. But, generally, cross-dressers only alter their gender appearance on specific occasions, while transgender individuals cultivate the opposite gender identity on a constant basis. It should also be noted, that "transvestite" has become a derogatory term as it has been lumped in with poor assessments of transgender as a mental disorder.

Transgender related topics as often been seen as personal issues whereby the individual expresses an inward urge to take up the gender of another.

There can be a confusion about the definitions of transgender and transsexual, as both terms have historically been used interchangeably. In most cases, "transgender" is used as an umbrella term for all "trans" people. And, depending on who you talk to, this is still accurate. Although, some people now prefer "trans" as the actual umbrella term, this article will give a brief overview of the terminology for better clarification.

A main way to clarify the trans terminology boils down to understanding that "gender" and "sex" are not the same thing. "Gender" refers to the societal identity of male or female. This is an anthropological definition based on the individual's societal "norms" for a gender. But "sex" refers to the actual reproductive organs/genitals. "Sex" is a biological definition that does not waiver from society to society. Some think of "sex" as meaning "intercourse," but this is not what the terminology is referring to.

Queer

This term includes a collection of gender identities and sexual identities. In time past, queer was used to insult and hurt people. Some people still take it as an offensive word, particularly those who have been called outin time past using the word. In recent times, it has been observed that some people use the term as a means if identifying themselves and they do this with pride.

However, it is important that you refer to someone as "queer" if you know that's how they identify themselves.

Transsexual

Going back to the breakdown of the terms, "trans" means "change" and "sexual" means "physical genitalia". Therefore, those who are transsexual are those that have been born with one type of sexual organs and wish to change them to the opposite sexual organs. This is most easily explained as people who feel they were "born into the wrong body." In another term, transsexual refers to the people whose current gender identity is contrast to the sex assigned to them at birth. Transsexuals seek out hormonal and/or surgical assistance to physically change their bodies to become the opposite sex of what they were born as. The process of transforming from one gender to another is called transitioning. The females who wish and desire to live as a man or who wishes to be recognized as a man is called female-to-male (FTM) trans men or transsexuals while males who wish to be recognized as females are called maleto-female (MTF) transsexuals or trans women.

There are different "levels" of transsexuals based on where they are in the transformation process from pre-operation to post. The main difference here is that transsexuals are not happy with the bodies they were born with and strive to physically change themselves to the opposite sex. This is beyond merely identifying as the opposite gender.

The Trans Community

When discussing the trans community and its definitions, a mention should be made about gays and lesbians. Remember, "trans" means change. Gays and lesbians are born with male or female genitalia and identify with their gender along the lines of societal norms. So a gay man is born with a penis, and also identifies himself in the society as a man. He is not trying to change anything about himself. The difference is that he is sexually attracted to males like himself. Although some may say, then, this is not a societal "norm." However, the point being made here is that none of these definitions have anything to do with sexual intercourse. The terminology refers to the physical sexual identity and the outward gender identity.

Chapter 2

Living the Life of a Transgender

According to psychology, studies have proven that these candidates are positive individuals who have great motives. Transgender individuals appreciate life and have made a choice of what they really want. Whether male or female, they have overcome the shadows of society and decided to take what belongs to them. They have come to appreciate human behavior and understand that a person can't really be happy unless they have a healthy reproductive system and gender identity that functions and complements their soul.

Transgender individuals spend a lot of time analyzing their gender expression and purpose in society. Due to this fact, by the time they undergo the change and become the gender they associate with, they become experts in that gender. They can also acknowledge the thoughts of others and reach out to those who feel they are abnormal or are deprived of what belongs to them by the course of nature. These individuals tend to be more sensitive to the doings of society in general, therefore giving them the ability to see things through that person's eyes. All in all, they are the most strong and courageous individuals, as they have managed to overcome the discrimination from society and sometimes have abandoned their loved ones so they can get shelter and peace of mind they want.

Many transgender individuals have expressed their frustration, feelings and have displayed courage in their attempts to ensure adequate protection and shielding themselves from this unnecessary abuse or discrimination and if they are so lucky, have communicated it through their writings. Some have sadly stated that they would rather die than face the harshness and pains inflicted by others based on what society dictates. This could be detrimental and may lead to suicide. This causes harassment, bullying, discrimination, mean-spirited and can lead to discord and this simply can not continue. The ignorance of others only motivate them to hurt and judge others just for their differences and what does that say for us as a people? What makes one person feel they are better than the other? We are all here and must learn to coexist and be more compassionate. How would you like it if the shoe was on the other foot? Not everything can be exactly defined as male only and female only. Life is far too complicated for that to ever happen and if that was the case then the world we live in would be quite boring.

Sometimes it is possible for a male to identify as a female or a female to identify as a male. It is not that inconceivable to be possible. Believe me, there are many more people than you may think that are transgender but for whatever reasons they just don't ever come out and they take it to the grave with them never really finding their inner peace or happiness.

That to me is a very sad and painful existence of feeling "trapped" and never being true to who you were inside and for no one to ever know the real you! That is why many transgender take their lives which is so very heartbreaking because it does not have to be that way!

The Role of the Transgender Community in the life of a Transgender Individual

Naturally, we are all identified as male or female by doctors when we are born. In the case of transgender individuals in the transgender community, this identification by other people may feel incorrect. They may identify more-so with the other sex. Remember, however, that a transgendered individual, regardless of being born as a male or female, may identify themselves as a heterosexual, homosexual or bisexual.

A common situation among transgender individuals is having been born with genitals of one gender and feeling that they are incomplete. They may feel pulled sexually, spiritually, or they simply may feel incomplete, based on the sex they have been born as. To help transgender individuals, most large cities in America have developed a strong community to help transgender people cope.

Since the boom of the internet, the transgender community has been able to grow and encourage a greater membership. They have been able to reach more people, conduct more thorough research, and develop more resources for their communities.

Through online avenues, transgender people are able to identify with other transgender stories, research and hear testimonials on transgender surgery, and ask questions to those who have been living a public transgender life. Since the popularity of chat rooms has emerged via the internet, transgender chat has allowed individuals to meet other people like them without revealing their privacy at the comfort their own home.

It is very easy to look at someone different from ourselves and judge them. It takes a much stronger and wiser person to understand them. Before judging the transgender personality, ask questions about the transgender community and research the internet to get to know who they really are. The simple truth of the matter is that we are all placed on this earth, and not one of us is just alike. Science has proven this several times and this is reason you would never find fingerprints that are alike. This is a wonderful and beautiful thing. That should be, and someday will be, recognized in a positive light by all.

Coming Out

Coming out is a term used to refer to LGBT people's acceptance, discovery and disclosure of their sexual orientation or gender identity.

Discovery of the 'Supporting LGBT Lives' Study 'Coming Out'

At 12 years of age, a person with LGBT life realises his or her identity

At 17 years of age. This is the perfect stage of disclosing one's LGBT identity to anyone

5 years. The duration of 5 years is the most common number of years that most young LGBT people hide their identity from others. This 5 year period coincides with school, puberty, and a critical period of emotion, social, and vocational development

The period prior to revealing one's identity (coming out) is particularly stressful because of fear of rejection by parents in particular, friends and because of isolation.

11

Chapter 3

The role of the media

Despite the political climate for the hot-button issue of gay marriage, the media has taken forward steps to increasing acceptance by portraying human relationships in alternative lifestyles. Additionally, there is a very strong community for gays, lesbians, bisexuals, and transgendered persons that can offer lots of support, if not in every town, then at least on the internet. Books, websites, television programs, and other media are offering more options geared to couples that break the heterosexual norm. Perhaps because the country is so divided by the issue, gay and lesbian relationships have received increased attention and debate in the past decade.

LGBT Mental Health and Suicidal Rate

Based on this study, 27% had self-harmed and 85% of these people did so more than once.

The first self-harmed is averagely at 16 years of age.

20% of males and 40% of females had self-harmed.

18% of LGBT people had attempted suicide and 85% classified their first attempt at suicide as related to stresses associated with their identity (e.g. fear of rejection by family or friends)

The average age of first suicide attempt was 17.5 years.

15% of males and 24% of females attempted suicide at least once.

About two-third of people aged 25 years and under had thought seriously about terminating their lives within the past year and over 50% had done so at some time.

The 3 most common LGBT-specific stresses identified were:

- fear of been rejected when contemplating on coming out;

- harassment and victimization experiences; and

- Negative school experiences.

Chapter 4

Gays and Lesbians

When questions are asked about who a gay or lesbian is, an answer can be as simple as a "Gay means when a man loves a man while a lesbian is a woman who is sexually and emotionally attracted to women." This holds true whether the woman is or has been married to a man, and whether she has had sex or a relationship with a woman. Complicated, right?

A lesbian is a woman who is emotionally, romantically and sexually attracted to women.

A gay is a man who is either emotionally, romantically or sexually attracted to men. The term gay can be used generally to refer to gay, lesbian, and bisexual people but most women prefer that the word lesbian is used to refer to their sexual orientation. Majority of the gay people do not like to be referred to as homosexuals because of the historical associations with the word which are mainly negative.

You'll find that many, if not most lesbian, have spent time in a relationship with men before coming out about their sexuality. That doesn't make them straight, it just makes them lesbians who came to their senses after being with guys for most part of their lives.

There's nothing quite as sweet as the feeling of freedom and accomplishment that comes along with coming out of the closet. You have eventually rid yourself of the burden of lies and hiding, and can now enjoy life as an openly gay person. This is a great achievement, as there are many people out there who take years to come out of the closet. And then of course there are those who never strike up the courage to be who they really are.

Gay and Lesbian Relationships

America has a reluctance to accept relationships between people of the same gender. This reluctance follows a similar pattern to the hostility towards interracial relationships. Although increasing, acceptance of gays, lesbians, bisexuals, and transgendered persons' relationships are now widespread in America today. The stereotype remains that these groups practice promiscuous lifestyles.

Many homosexuals currently seek marriage rights in order to recognize their committed relationships. This campaign for gay marriage rights has been met with acceptance and hostility. Several states recently voted to revise the wording for legal marriages so that a marriage can only exist between a man and a woman. In addition, several states have witnessed court decisions legalizing same sex marriage. The issue is very polarizing in America, and the opposition to gay marriage is largely based on religious, moral, and cultural beliefs. In order to defuse some of this polarization, some states have found middle ground in recognizing "civil unions" for same sex couples.

Responsibilities of Gays and Lesbians

The gay and lesbian community has for a long while been ostracized for a condition that many feel they are born with. While some may make a conscious decision to abandon the so-called "normal" heterosexual relationships for a walk on the LGBT side, many feel it is part of who they are as much as their hearts are integral to their bodies. Genetic research has lent a lot of credibility to this belief, and has also helped to change the way in which gays are viewed by the public at large. But while conditions are better now than they were 100 years ago, this group of people still has a long way to go in the world at large. To continue to make strides forward, gays have the following responsibilities to their respective communities.

Gays and lesbians must protect the young. When a child becomes a man (or woman), he (or she) struggles to define who they really are and who they are going to become. Teenagers are particularly susceptible to bullying and abuse, and it has led to some pretty tragic consequences. Younger generations are becoming more accepting of the gay and lesbian lifestyle. It is important to keep this momentum going by making the public aware of what a gay teen goes through. By promoting respect early in life, gays and lesbians of today stand to make the world of tomorrow a much better place.

The GLBT community must continue to fight for equal rights. The world does not give gays and lesbians an equal playing field. Many societies still look at it as "sinful" or even "criminal." In the U.S., gays have had a long history of being denied civil rights such as serving in the military or raising children. It is important that members of the GLBT community continue to get involved in politics in their community and the world at large.

Gays and lesbians must work to change unhealthy and untrue stereotypes. Religious zealots have long called the gay and lesbian community "depraved" and "sexually charged" without acknowledging their humanity. By forming normal friendships with "straight" people and allowing them to see that you're a person just like them, you will be surprised at how quickly change occurs.

The GLBT community must not succumb to the "us versus them" mentality. While denial of civil rights can quickly charge an issue and lead to negative emotions, it is important to remember and respect the individual. The relationships you forge with those who are different from you are and will remain the greatest tool that you have to overcome prejudice, bigotry, and violence. Gays and lesbians must not resort to trampling on the rights of others as theirs have too often been trampled upon. By being the difference, you can make a difference.

Lesbian, Gay, Bisexual and Transgender (LGBT) people in the workplace

LGBT people tend to be invisible in the workplace. They often mask their identity for fear of job discrimination which in turn leads to the underreporting of discrimination. Majority are not been informed during job interviews if they would employ a LGBT personality. On employment, they hand over the company rules to them and yet they do not find it stated in there. For them not to be discriminated against or lose their job, they keep this to themselves.

Now, the question is why do LGBT people not want to disclose their identity? Perhaps, this could be that they won't be able to handle other people's reactions and coming out of the closet may increase the likelihood of being the target of discrimination. They weigh up the pros and cons of coming out, such as greater personal authenticity, political and social empowerment, more open and potentially more productive relationships with colleagues' and freedom from the need to devote energy to the fear of discovery and all that may entail.

Consequently, researchers have conceptualized coming out as a "recurring, rational decision-making process that LGBT individuals undertake each time they encounter new persons and new situations and that requires the assessment of the potential benefits and costs (Rostosky & Riggle 2000).

Factors that might influence a person "coming out" include good coping resources, the presence of non-discrimination policies in the person and his/her partner's workplace and the presence of LGBT support networks. Interestingly, team composition also plays a vital role - LGBT people in work teams composed primarily of men, that are not racially balanced or have male supervisors report experiencing more homophobia and discrimination. It is a big decision for employees whether or not to invite their partners to company social events and in reality, this is probably only done where the organization is tolerant of LGBT persons.

There are two main concerns about LBGTs in workplaces. One cause for concern is the impact of sexual prejudice on their career and the other relates to the impact of anti-gay prejudice on career proficiency. Anti-gay activists see teaching as a contested area because they believe that children are at risk of "normalising the homosexual lifestyle". Personally, I do not agree with this because homosexuals are really just the same as heterosexuals in everything except their sexual habits. They buy houses and pay their mortgages and worry about debt like everyone else. Just as heterosexuals will not exhibit sexual behaviour in public, neither do homosexuals.

Some people do not agree with gays in the military, perhaps they are afraid that a gay partner will in some way get access to security clearance. I think that this is an invalid argument because homosexuals have taken an oath to the Head of State and to the people and they are equally bound to respect national security.

On the other side of the coin, it is possible that LGBT people will be affected by homophobic people in the public service e.g. social workers, lawyers, and teachers. The popular film "Philadelphia" depicted homophobic attorneys but it is rare to see this in film or in the media.

Ways of combating homophobia in the workplace

The trade union congress launched a new guide recently for union representatives in all work places across the country on ways to combat homophobia in the workplace. This guide was launched in September 2013, *LGBT Equality at Work*. This guide presents the legal instructions for facing harrssment at place of work and guided advice on how union reps can represent their members in the appropriate ways.

The trade union congress believes the guide will help unions to make the work areas more accepting fot transgers and LGBT to work.

Despite this guide, some still face prejudice at work and it's important that homophobia is tackled when and where it happens.

However, the best way of combating homophobia in the workplace is by training employees regarding prejudice, communication and diversity.

Chapter 5

LGBT Relationships

Gay Dating, Lifestyle and Personal

Majority came out to mostly a friend or another trusted personalty before coming out to their family. Everyone - friends and family, and mostly parents in particular, have a crucial role to play in supporting LGBT people as they come out. This encouragement and support can act as a means of protection against specific stresses LGBT young people may come across in school such as homophobic bullying.

The popularity of gay lifestyle is understood from the number of gay dating websites that has sprung up on the Internet this days. It is a very good platform for closeted gays to contact gay males for gay romance, love and sexual relationship as anyone else would wish for.

Gay Personal

Out Personals and Queer - These words characterize the gay lifestyle, which till today is not an accepted mode of life to a large populace on this planet. Even in modern, fast-paced societies where liberal attitudes and sexual liberation are a norm, gay men are looked down upon. Gay activity is sneered or frowned upon and they are looked down as queers or out personals.

Social Life

Country politics and social caretakers' indulge in raging discussions on gay relationship and gay rights in discussion forums, parliament, and conventions. There is a marked hesitancy in accepting gays in government services and other public enterprises, though some nations have accorded acceptance but more has to be done. In many instance, persons discovered as following gay lifestyle have been debarred from social circles and offices.

The crux is that homosexuality is in practice since the early ages and it is still as popular, without any signs of receding or vanishing from the face of earth. Then why not accept it since it does not infringe on anyone's privacy or way of life. It is not in any way detrimental to the society since gay dating lifestyle is a much-closeted practice.

I am not arguing for gay life as a gay-which I am not-but what I want to stress is that everyone has a right to express his or her sexuality and practice as long as it does not hurt others.

Why Gay?

The reason behind sneer or ridicule of gay lifestyle is that it is a biological variance as sex is for procreation and a man-to-man sex does not give birth to new being. But then, anal sex practice is not limited to gay couples only, it is much practiced by straight couples too, so what are we saying? Any way, gay romance and love is a very strong force that binds the gay couple together sometimes in permanent relationship.

Sex is for procreation but it is for pleasure too, and any which way you can. Therefore, "Out" sex practice is not restricted to guys only but rather practiced by straight lifestyle followers in some way or the other. So live and let live.

Gay Parenting

Somewhere between 6 million and 12 million children are blessed with gay parents. Yet, gay and lesbian parents continue to struggle on a daily basis with the challenges of a homophobic society and institutionalized oppression. Gay's and lesbians are the only population facing restrictions on the rights and privileges of parenthood.

When it comes to parenting, as well as other civil rights, gays and lesbians are de facto second class citizens:

1) Many states still bar adoptions and foster parenting by gay men and lesbians;

2) Family courts have taken children away from gay parents' and awarded custody to a heterosexual relative or former spouse;

3) Excessive custodial and visitation restrictions are also part of the gay parenting experience;

4) Hard to place and chronically ill children are often the only available adoption options for gay parents;

5) Legal limitations on same-sex partnership protection, such as shared health insurance, parental leave, etc, put an extra burden on gay parents and their co-parenting partners;

6) Social deprivation in all the ways in which gay relationships are not supported in this society, in families of origin, school, church, and state, contribute to the stress and constriction experienced by gay and lesbian families

The Role of Research on Gay Parenting

Despite social and legal obstacles, lesbians and gays have often succeeded in creating and sustaining meaningful family and parental relationships. An American Psychological Association review of extensive research evidence dating back to 40 years found out that, there appears to be no disadvantage rendered to children raised by gays and lesbians, and instead may result in several distinctive enhancements. For example, children of lesbian or gay parent's showed increased empathy and tolerance for differences.

Research on gay parenting has been in the forefront of the process of dismantling mistaken assumptions, both legal and cultural, facing gay parents that have been expressed in judicial opinions, legislative initiatives, or public policies relevant to lesbian and gay parents and their children. Thus, many studies have been conducted to evaluate the accuracy of negative expectations about lesbian and gay parents or about their children.

The Effect of Gay Parenting on Children

Research studies on children in gay or lesbian households unanimously assert that the sexual orientation of moms or dads has no impact on their kids' sexuality, gender identity, or any other aspect of their psychological and emotional development. Not surprisingly, a recent paper published in the American Sociological Review reveales that, while the emotional and mental health of youngsters with heterosexual or gay parents is essentially the same, the offspring of lesbians and gays are more likely to accept non-traditional gender roles and are more tolerant of same-sex relationships. Teenage boys were more sexually restrained than peers from heterosexual households and were likely to be more nurturing and affectionate than their counterparts in heterosexual families. Daughters of lesbians were more likely not to conform to sex-typed roles, showing greater interest in activities and occupations that are not traditionally female. Children of gays and lesbians also formed friendship bonds with their peers as easily as kids of heterosexuals, despite the harassment and teasing they were subjected to. Daughters of lesbians tended to have higher self-esteem, and sons were more caring and less aggressive relative to peers from heterosexual households. A 1994 study conducted by Charlotte Patterson revealed that children of lesbians exhibited "a greater overall sense of well-being" than kids of heterosexuals, perhaps because their moms forced fewer "sex-typed" preferences upon them. Indeed most problems that daughters and sons of lesbian, gay, and bisexual parents are said to have, actually stem from going through a divorce, and not from parents' sexual orientation. There is no evidence that these children face any more difficulties socializing in school than children of straight parents. Gay children are exposed to more people of the opposite sex than many kids of straight parents and, there is no evidence to suggest that this is harmful. Accordingly, if these children identify as lesbian, gay, or bisexual, they are likely to be much better off than lesbian, gay and bisexual children of straight parents.

Lesbian Parenting

"Take this time of preparation to deeply reflect on partnership-not only do you need to share your own childhood stories and reflect on their impact on each other, but also discuss what you might call your 'parenting mission statement' or philosophy."-Barbara Nicholson and Lysa Parker, Attached at the Heart: 8 Proven Parenting Principles for Raising Connected and Compassionate Children

How Do You Intend to Parent?

What is your opinion about the following issues? These are issues couples need to decide on together.

1) How will the partner carrying the child nurture herself and the baby during pregnancy? As you discuss on who will do what, this would be the time to discuss things like healthy eating and exercise during pregnancy or managing stress, as well as any health concerns one or the other of you may have.

2) Does any of you find it easier to eat well or exercise? Studies have shown that exercising regularly can reduce the likelihood of premature delivery by 50% or more.

3) Decide on where you would want to have the baby? What are your opinions about having an OB-GYN or midwife or doula or all three?

4) Home birth or hospital? Natural delivery or not? Which would the carrier prefer? Will both partners be in the delivery room or together at the home birth?

"Attachment parenting advocates know that the most beneficial birth choice is the one that has the fewest interventions and allows for the mother and baby to be awake, aware and able to connect during and after the birth." -- Barbara Nicholson and Lysa Parker, Attached at

the Heart: 8 Proven Parenting Principles for Raising
Connected and Compassionate Children

5) Do you want to bottle feed or breastfeed?

Most people know that breastfeeding is good for the
baby's health and is recommended for that reason, but are
you also aware that it enhances and increases the
emotional bond between mother and child. One way to
increase and enhance the bond for the non-breastfeeding
mother is to have lots of skin-to-skin contact with the
baby.

6) Will you consider circumcision if you should have a
boy?

"There is a considerable evidence that newborns who are
circumcised without analgesia experience pain and
physiologic stress. Neonatal physiologic responses to
circumcision pain include changes in heart rate, blood
pressure, and oxygen saturation," -American Academy of
Pediatrics.

Based on these finding, they do not recommend the
procedure, but stated that if parents do decide to
circumcise, it should be done with the use of a local
anesthetic.

7) What about vaccinations? All? Some? or none at all?

This decision is such an important one and one that often
generates strong feelings in one way or the other. Those
who express concern about vaccines are often concerned,
specifically, about the additives used in vaccines and the

possibility that they play a causal role in some of the medical problems infants and children experience after vaccination. It's your choice, so choode wisely.

8) What will you do if your baby gets sick? Is one of you more inclined toward natural or holistic parenting and the other more conventional? Responsibility of nurturing and taking care of the baby should be carried out by both parties.

9) If there be any new disagreements that surfaced as you discussed these additional questions, discuss on how best to resolve these differences?

Chapter 6

Positive Pregnancy and Birth

Research suggests that some of the determining factors involved in having a positive pregnancy and birth experience are the quality of the relationship between partners, the presence or lack of support throughout the pregnancy and birth experience and the reductions of fears and anxiety during the process.

Developing a parenting philosophy, and plan that addresses these concerns and any need for healing in the relationship or from childhood or other past issues is the best way to create what is needed for a positive beginning for the children you bring into the world.

Bisexual

A bisexual is someone (man or woman) who is sexually and emotionally attracted to both men and women and who may feel comfortable pursuing a relationship with either one. Note, if you've had sex with a man in the past — and even if you've enjoyed it — that doesn't necessarily mean you are bisexual (or in turn, that you are not a lesbian).

Most of us would get off if we were making out with a reasonably attractive partner (if you know what I mean). What matters is whether you truly are attracted to that person as a woman or man and whether you would be happy and fulfilled in a relationship with either sex.

There is a lot of confusion about the concept of bisexuality. Many people are 100% gay or lesbian, in other words they are sexually and emotionally attracted only to partners of the same sex. Others are completely heterosexual, bonding in sexual and intimate relationships only with people of another sex. But what about everybody else? A significant percentage of people do not fit neatly into either of these categories, because they experience sexual and emotional attractions and feelings for people of different genders at some point during their lives.

For lack of a better term, they are called bisexuals. Many people hate this term, for a variety of reasons, and prefer to call themselves ''pansexual,'' ''non-preferential,'' ''sexually fluid'', ''ambisexual,'' or simply ''queer.'' This is particularly true for young people under the age of 40, who consider the term ''bisexual'' to be outdated and limiting, and do not identify with this label at all.

Most people think that bisexuality is a state of confusion, that it's a straight person on his or her way to being gay or vice versa. The truth is, bisexuality is a valid sexual orientation on its own.

Bisexuality is different from bi-curiosity. Bi-curious people are usually heterosexuals who are interested in "experimentation" with homosexuality. They are merely looking to try it and nothing more. Although some bi-curious people do end up bisexual, bi-curiosity doesn't exactly equate to bisexuality. There are also bi-permissive people. These people are generally heterosexual, but they claim to be open to pursuing a relationship with members of the same-sex.

Unlike homosexuality, bisexuality doesn't seem so disreputable in the eyes of society. There are even ancient cultures wherein bisexuality was the norm, and it wasn't seen as a problem as long as they eventually married someone of the opposite sex. Although bisexuality doesn't seem so disreputable in the eyes of most heterosexuals, the gay and lesbian community sees it differently. Most (not all) gays and lesbians view bisexuality as a stage of indecision. Sometimes, they even see bisexuals as people who are in denial of their own homosexuality. In fact, there's a joke that goes "Bi now, gay later." Even if some bisexuals do end up being homosexual, this isn't a common occurrence.

Usually, both homosexuals and heterosexuals have problems going out with bisexuals. They seem to fear that if they date a bisexual, they will be abandoned when the bisexual "switches sides". Because of prevalent biphobia, most bisexuals have problems or issues when dating. However, because of the invention of the internet, bisexuals can go to online dating sites to find other bisexuals or people who wouldn't mind dating bisexuals.

According to Alfred Kinsey, a famous researcher on human sexual behavior, sexuality isn't exclusively homosexual or heterosexual. Kinsey said the sexuality was actually a continuum between these two extremes, and that it is only the human mind that labels human sexuality so rigidly. Most bisexuals definitely agree with this philosophy, saying that they fall in love with the person and not the gender.

Bisexual Dating

There was a time when bisexuality wasn't even considered a legitimate sexual orientation. However, over the years, people started considering the bisexual society as real and authentic. This trend eventually gave rise to the concept of online bisexual dating sites, which would provide a platform where people from all walks of life could connect with each other, explore their sexuality and find a compatible partner.

Have you ever asked yourself what bisexual dating offers that conventional dating doesn't?

Bisexual dating sites seem to have completely eliminated the hardships that bisexual singles had to face. For instance, these sites made it possible for them to connect with like-minded singles from across the globe without having to explain their sexuality or sexual preferences. Given the fact that such websites are dominated with people with similar interests, finding a person who understands you isn't a herculean task.

Other benefits of bisexual dating sites

1. Avenue for you to connect with more people: It goes without saying that online dating platforms have more users than what you'd be able to connect with in the real world. As a matter of fact, this is one of the main reasons behind the remarkable success of dating sites over the last decade and a half. Leading dating sites made for

bisexual singles have anywhere between 500,000 and 700,000 members, which provides immense scope if you're looking to make friends or find true love.

2. Advanced privacy options: Dating sites require your personal information in order to deliver a more personalized user experience. This information also helps users connect with like - minds based on their unique preferences. Therefore, leading dating companies do not take any chances with security that could eventually lead to data theft or misuse of information. Besides, dating sites allow users to interact with other users' without having to share their contact information.

3. Helps to save time and money: Gone are the days when you had to waste a great deal of time as well as money heading out on dates at fancy restaurants and coffee shops with people whom you were introduced by a common friend. Dating sites give users the unique opportunity to communicate with fellow users online, courtesy of options such as emailing and instant messaging. Some websites also supports advanced communication options like video chat and online calling, taking the whole experience to a new level altogether.

All in all, it goes without saying that online bisexual dating have managed to revolutionize the way bisexual singles interacted with like - minded singles and formed relationships.

Roles of Mental Health Staff

The following guidance outlines the steps that health care providers can take at ensuring that services are provided in an inclusive way to LGBT service users as well as their partners and families.

1: Respect the rights of LGBT service users. You are not to discriminate on the basis of sexual orientation or gender identity. Use language and questions that reflect openness; it is of utmost importance that you do not try to assume and recognize that gender identity may differ from presentation.

2: Empathic relationships and respecting others opinion are required between people using the mental health service and those providing them.

LGBT-inclusive service is a service that respects values of both users and service providers. As a health care staff, you are to respond supportively when service users disclose their identity. You can ask the person about their experience of coming out and if there have issues related to being LGBT that they would like to discuss with you or need help with.

Ensure to familiarise yourself with LGBT issues such as difficulties before or after coming out, homophobic or transphobic bullying, isolation, and lack of family support.

For health care staff working in Child and Adolescent Mental Health Services, recognise when working with young people that issues related to sexual orientation or gender identity can play a role in young people's presentation   with emotional and behavioural issues.

Also, recognize that when working with older LGBT people, they may have fears and anxieties related to historical approaches to LGBT people and their relationships.

3: Provision of a holistic service and full continuum of care should be provide

Most health services are likely to have LGBT service users or family members or parents who are LGBT. In a recent study, about 8% of people were identified as bisexual, lesbian or gay. This therefore follows that a similar percentage of mental health service users are LGBT.

A person's identity may not be associated to their need for the service. For some their experiences as an LGBT person will be closely related to their presentation. Therefore, in addition to general assessment and treatment, consider the role of LGBT-specific stresses in the person's presentation to services, including questioning their gender identity, fear of coming out, lack of support after coming out or, for those who are already 'out', experiences such   as homophobic or transphobic bullying.

Mental health staff should be aware of the LGBT people's specific needs and the category of LGBT community resources and organisations that can be used in recovery programmes.

4: Operate a quality environment that promotes good health and upholds the security and safety of service users

5. Access to services. Mental health services must ensure equality in access to their service regardless of the service

user's gender, sexual orientation, civil status, family status, age, disability, ethnicity, social class, religion or membership of the traveler community.

6: Provide advice, information and support to the partners of LGBT service users in the same way you would to the partners of heterosexual people.

7: Display LGBT information. Create a safe environment where staff should be mindful of the safety and security of LGBT individuals who may be subjected to negative comments or behaviour related to their LGBT identity from other service users.

CONCLUSION

Accurate and imaginary scientific research report can and do have effect on our personal decisions and self understanding, and can contribute to the public conversation, including political and cultural debates.

Although the society posits a stigma on these set of people, with love, we can bring them to us and help them to overcome their fears.

There is need for an extensive recreation of our existence.

Our perspective of sexual irientation and dexual identity needs to conform with what God has ordained it to be.

Whatever circumstance you may have found yourself, please know that Jesus is ever so merciful and will accept you just the way you are. However, we need a re-orientation of heart and a genuine one at that.

We need to follow the ordained plan of God, discover ourselves and seek out the help, guidance and support we need.

NOTE: *The LGBT Equality at Work* is available free to unions and can be downloaded from the TUC website at:

http://www.tuc.org.uk/equality/tuc-22599-f0.cfm

END

Thank you for reading my book. If you enjoyed it, won't you please take a moment to look at my other titles?

Thanks!

Lauren A. McMann

www.ingramcontent.com/pod-product-compliance
Lightning Source LLC
Chambersburg PA
CBHW060817260726
48660CB00002B/996